⌐FRAMEABLES⌐

◆

21 nature prints
for a picture-perfect home

DEYROLLE
French Botanical Art

Flammarion

Observation

The introduction to this work is being written during a virtually unique moment in the modern history of humanity. By chance, dear readers, my recent activities have led me to being confined, alone, in a small log cabin in the rice fields of Alentejo, in Portugal, facing the ocean. The only company I have is an omnipresent nature, with its flurries of storks, herons, egrets, spoonbills, black ibises, or else its beetles rummaging away in the sandy soil. Meanwhile, in almost perfect equilibrium, I have set about preparing the kitchen garden that will feed my family, who will come to join me, as soon as this becomes possible. I think of my son, Théodore, who is just one year old, and will—I hope—grow up in a world of cooperation and sharing, of preservation and communication. People will certainly remind him of 2020, a special year that will surely raise at least slightly our heavy veil, and so guide us back toward the essential! *Feeding ourselves, learning, understanding, dreaming, marveling, and communicating.*

All I can wish for him, and for all the world's children, both big and small, is to be as close as possible to this basic need to understand Life. The life that feeds us, takes care of us, and reassures once we have understood its workings. To do so, we need to take the time to look, we need to *observe, to frame* in our minds everything about it that is beautiful, practical, pleasant, and effervescent.

Deyrolle's plates, which have provided the drawings published in this book, began to be produced almost 150 years ago when, in France, free public education brought the natural sciences to the attention of a new generation of schoolchildren and citizens. These drawings still exude the scent of the soil, the warmth of dawn, the rustling of leaves, the way a farmer senses with his hands the promise of his crops, the fertility of the living world, and our joys. As we grow familiar with these drawings, *framed* on our walls, we hear their voices telling us about an invisible world. Taking the time to look at them, and observe them, should allow us to look at our own life, all the better to transcend it.

I would like Deyrolle's drawings to become once more a place where we can store our nourishment, knowledge, and happiness. Observe them, frame them, share them. Then let us thank the naturalists because, today more than ever, they make our eyes and hearts want to be committed players in the mystery of Life.

Louis Albert de Broglie

Brejos da Carregueir
de Baixo, March 26, 2020

ARBRES

PEUPLIER
Populus pyramidalis (Salicaceæ)

BOULEAU
Betula alba (Castaneaceæ)

FIGUIER
Ficus carica (Artocarpeæ)

CHÊNE
Quercus robur (Cupuliferæ)

SAPIN
Abies pectinata (Coniferæ)

SAULE
Salix babylonica (Salicaceæ)

OLIVIER
Olea europæa (Oleineæ)

YUCCA EN ARBRE
Yucca arborescens (Liliaceæ)

POIRIER
Pyrus communis (Rosaceæ)

EUCALYPTUS
Eucalyptus globulus (Myrtaceæ)

PIN MARITIME
Pinus maritima (Coniferæ)

PALMIER
Livistona australis (Coryphineæ)

FOUGÈRE ARBORESCENTE
Dicksonia antarctica (Filiceæ)

HÊTRE
Fagus sylvatica (Cupuliferæ)

DRAGONNIER
Dracœna draco (Dracœneæ)

RAVENALA
Ravenala madagascariensis (Musaceæ)

ARAUCARIE
Araucaria imbricata (Coniferæ)

UNONA
Polyalthia asiatica (Anonaceæ)

ARBRE BOUTEILLE
Brachychiton Delabacki (Sterculiaceæ)

Mobilier et Matériel pour l'Enseignement. — LES FILS D'ÉMILE DEYROLLE, 46, Rue du Bac, Paris

Trees

Botanical plate no. 229
Late nineteenth–
early twentieth century

"Teaching Supplies and Material"
Éditions Les Fils d'Émile Deyrolle
46 rue du Bac, 7th arr., Paris
Imprimerie Gaillac-Monrocq & Cie

This exceptional plate by Émile Deyrolle's sons offers us a trip around the world. It is a journey of nineteen stages, depicting the same number of tree species. Shown all on the same scale (even though some, such as the eucalyptus, can grow to a hundred feet or thirty meters high), and drawn face-on—the better to depict their structures and their identities—they each display their own unique feeling of grace. From Africa to Europe, from Asia to the Caucasus, from Australia to Hawaii, and from Mexico to Madagascar, a map of the world has been placed on a single page. Some, like the *unona*, an African tree with fruit-like peppercorns, no longer bear the same names, and to find a trace of them it is necessary to explore eighteenth-century handbooks. Others, such as the dragon tree, are on the tragic list of endangered species. While it may seem to be an attractive idea to make matches or cheese boxes out of poplar wood, the life of a tree can also change the life of a human. "Look at the light in the olive trees. It is as brilliant as a diamond," exclaimed the painter Auguste Renoir. Out of love for the shifting shadows and light of an olive grove that was doomed to disappear, he acquired a property in the South of France and had his studio built there.

But, no matter how different their morphologies might be, a tree is still a tree. They are all structured according to the same principle: a stalk, pointed upward, which bears leaves. This trunk, which for a young oak starts out with a diameter of barely an inch, will become several feet wide after a few years. It provides the communication between the roots and the leaves. It is the tree's conductive organ, routing the nourishment taken from the earth, then deploying it from one leaf to the next, to feed this magnificent living organism. These stalks might go by different names—trunk, bole, or woody stem—depending on the type of tree, but they all contain nourishment conserved out of sight, for when times are hard.

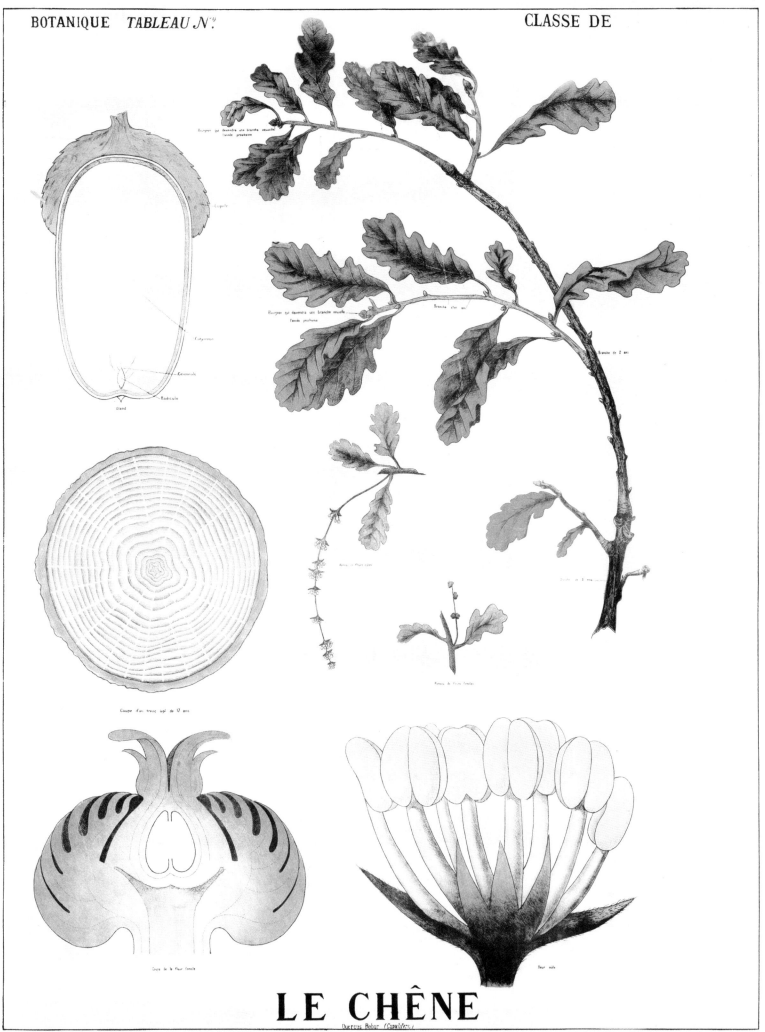

LE CHÊNE

Quercus Robur (Cupulifera)

Edité à Paris par Emile DEYROLLE Naturaliste 23 Rue de la Monnaie

The Oak
Quercus robur
(Cupulifers)

Botanical plate
Second half of the nineteenth century
Éditions Émile Deyrolle
23 rue de la Monnaie, 1st arr., Paris

In his constant concern to teach science in all its detail, Émile Deyrolle set about clearly showing the different concentric layers of the trunk, which reveal a tree's age. Just seventeen short years for the oak depicted here—barely the beginning of childhood for certain specimens, which can live to more than 1,000 years old.

In the top left-hand corner of the image, the acorn, with its cupule on the top, looks rather like a bewigged magistrate. Acorns are much liked by pigs, whose flesh they naturally flavor, but they are also suitable for human consumption in terrines or sweet tarts, though this requires meticulous preparation due to their high concentration of tannin.

The wood of the oak, known for its resistance, was long used to build warships, while its smooth, grayish bark was employed to tan leather.

"I call by their names the trees on my path, I touch with love their branches with my hand," wrote the poet Lamartine tenderly.

On this plate, intended to educate children, young shoots with their sinuous branches and smooth, gleaming bark bend their heads to reveal filaments bearing stamens. It is in springtime, at the moment when the leaves are reborn, that we see these "catkins," or male flowers. A few days later, the female flowers with pistils emerge on the new branches, surrounded by a large number of scales that form the cupule, which will later enclose the fruit. As though through the lens of a microscope, the artist has reproduced side by side these two varieties, borne by the same tree. It is a way of emphasizing the lingering question as to how such a mighty colossus can be born from so tiny a seed.

TABLEAUX
D'HISTOIRE NATURELLE
par
M. GASTON BONNIER
Professeur à la Sorbonne
Membre de l'Académie des Sciences

N° 751

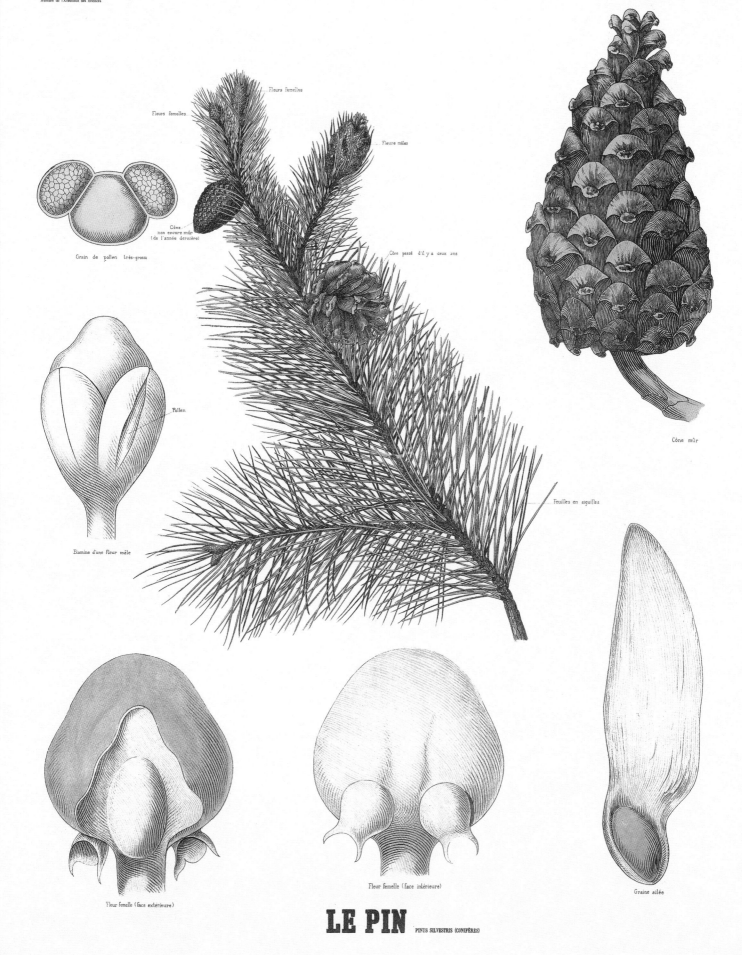

Fleurs femelles

Fleurs femelles

Fleurs mâles

Cône
non encore mûr
(de l'année dernière)

Grain de pollen très-grossi

Cône passé d'il y a deux ans

Pollen

Feuilles en aiguilles

Étamine d'une fleur mâle

Cône mûr

Fleur femelle (face extérieure)

Fleur femelle (face intérieure)

Graine ailée

LE PIN
PINUS SILVESTRIS (CONIFÈRES)

Établissements DEYROLLE, Éditeurs, 46, Rue du Bac, Paris 7e

The Pine
Pinus sylvestris
(Conifers)

Natural history plate
no. 751
Late nineteenth–
early twentieth century

By Gaston Bonnier,
professor at the Sorbonne
and member of the Académie des Sciences
Établissements Deyrolle, Éditeurs
46 rue du Bac, 7th arr., Paris
Imprimerie Gaillac-Monrocq & Cie

Each spring, a cloud of yellow dust escapes from the flowers of the Scots pine. While anyone who fears seasonal allergies avoids these abundant outbursts of pollen, this gift offered by the *Pinus sylvestris* is a delight for bees. As a tree growing in mountainous regions—resisting both summer heat and cold winters, from Siberia to Spain—its needles provide an essential oil used in the treatment of respiratory diseases. Meanwhile its sap, mixed with honey, is used in the Vosges region of France to make its renowned cough drops.

Signed by Gaston Bonnier (1853–1922)—a botanist and member of the Académie des Sciences—this typical nineteenth-century natural-history plate marries educative clarity with simple aesthetics. Spread out over the page around a pine branch with its immediately recognizable "needles" and "cones," the blossoms and seeds draw our eyes in due course. With a few delicate strokes, this great professor from the University of the Sorbonne, and founder of its botanical research laboratory, attracts our attention.

First, there are the small, deep-ocher male catkins. Then come the female flowers—shaped like little cones—which have been carefully drawn both ways, inside and out. The drawing is both meticulous and crafted, with the flowers carefully placed on the tips of the boughs. Bonnier instilled scientific information, without overdoing it. He thus showed that two years of fruit are required—those well-known pointed cones—before maturity is reached. These long seeds will then break away, to be blown by the winds and take root.

The pine cone was a major feature of art nouveau, before being stylized by the art deco movement. It appeared on ceramics, sculpted decorations, and cast-iron gates. Émile Gallé—a master glassmaker and founder of the Nancy School—as well as René Lalique—who, at the 1900 Paris World's Fair, displayed a stunning *Dog's Collar* with a pine-cone pattern and golden needles—both regenerated the decorative arts, by drawing from this naturalistic source.

PLANTES

FEUILLES

La feuille est l'organe des fonctions essentielles de la plante :
respiration, assimilation (nutrition), transpiration

FEUILLES SIMPLES

FEUILLES COMPOSÉES

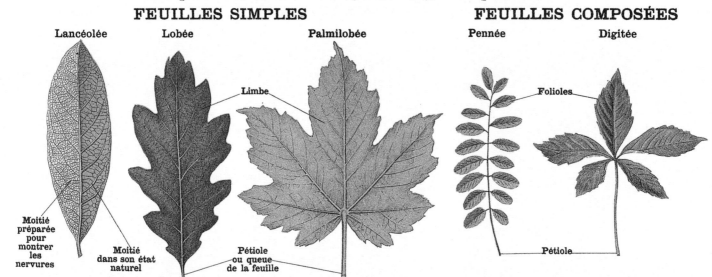

Lancéolée — Lobée — Palmilobée — Pennée — Digitée

Limbe — Folioles

Moitié préparée pour montrer les nervures — Moitié dans son état naturel — Pétiole ou queue de la feuille — Pétiole

Sur la feuille existent de petites saillies, appelées nervures ;
ces nervures sont l'organe de la circulation de la sève

La feuille composée est formée de feuilles secondaires,
ou folioles, réunies par un pétiole commun

Mobilier et Matériel pour l'Enseignement. — LES FILS D'ÉMILE DEYROLLE, 46. rue du Bac, Paris (7ᵉ)

PLANTES

FLEURS

La fleur est l'ensemble des organes qui produisent la graine

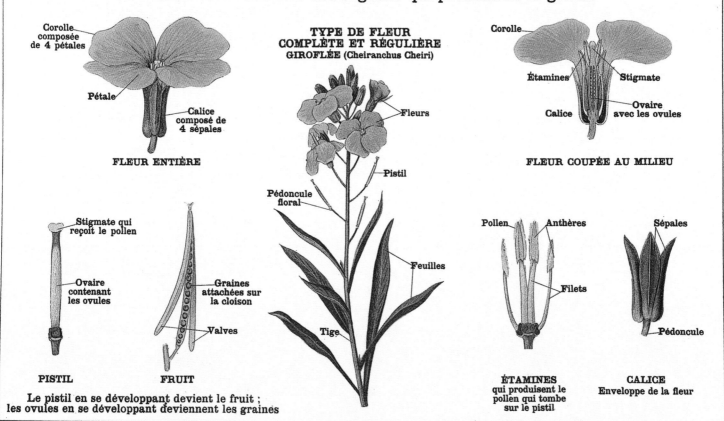

Corolle composée de 4 pétales

Pétale

Calice composé de 4 sépales

FLEUR ENTIÈRE

TYPE DE FLEUR
COMPLÈTE ET RÉGULIÈRE
GIROFLÉE (Cheiranchus Cheiri)

Fleurs

Pistil

Pédoncule floral

Feuilles

Tige

Corolle

Étamines — Stigmate

Calice — Ovaire avec les ovules

FLEUR COUPÉE AU MILIEU

Stigmate qui reçoit le pollen

Ovaire contenant les ovules

Graines attachées sur la cloison

Valves

Pollen — Anthères

Filets

Sépales

Pédoncule

PISTIL   **FRUIT**

Le pistil en se développant devient le fruit ;
les ovules en se développant deviennent les graines

ÉTAMINES
qui produisent le pollen qui tombe sur le pistil

CALICE
Enveloppe de la fleur

Mobilier et Matériel pour l'Enseignement. — LES FILS D'ÉMILE DEYROLLE, 46. rue du Bac, Paris (7ᵉ)

Plants
–
Leaves

Botanical plate no. 9
Late nineteenth–
early twentieth century

"Teaching Supplies and Material"
Éditions Les Fils d'Émile Deyrolle
46 rue du Bac, 7th arr., Paris
Imprimerie Gaillac-Monrocq & Cie

Laid out on the page at distances allowing for no overlapping—as in the production of an herbal—the leaves have been neatly lined up, with no indication of their species. They each have their own contours and particularities, shades of green and plays of transparency, either simple or composed. However, they all share a common point: a flat element—called a blade—attached by an extension, or petiole, to the stalk.

A leaf's blade is a form of skin. As in the human body, it is a tissue that exposes a network of vessels and allows the plant to feed. There is no blood, but a diet made up of green matter—or chlorophyll—is directed to the nerve endings. Plants share another characteristic with mankind. They breathe and thus absorb oxygen, while giving off carbonic acid. But this is twinned with the ability to assimilate carbon from the air and dispel oxygen. Quite a marvel!

Plants
–
Flowers

Botanical plate no. 9
Late nineteenth–
early twentieth century

"Teaching Supplies and Material"
Éditions Les Fils d'Émile Deyrolle
46 rue du Bac, 7th arr., Paris
Imprimerie Gaillac-Monrocq & Cie

The almost ocher-yellow wallflower depicted here is a plant that—as its name suggests—particularly appreciates the walls and roofs of houses, as well as balconies and flowerbeds. It is one of the first flowers to bring color back to the world after winter. If you plunge your nose between its four cross-shaped petals, you will smell its fine scent. You will also notice the elegance of its dense, green, lanceolate leaves, and delightful luminous presence.

However, Émile Deyrolle's descendants did not choose the wallflower for aesthetic reasons. It was selected as a good example of a "complete flower," in which the pistils and stamens are united in the same organ. The plate's perfect details display the composition of the flower and its life cycle. Starting as a bud, it blooms to reveal its calyx, corolla, stamen, and pistil. Once the flowers have wilted, the pistil alone remains, before drying out to release its seeds, born from a transformation of the ovules. We are then free to sow them aplenty.

FRUITS

GOYAVE
Psidium pyriferum *(Myrtaceas)*

AVOCAT
Persea gratissima *(Lauraceas)*

CITRON
Citrus limon *(Rutaceas)*

ANANAS
Ananassa sativa *(Bromeliaceas)*

BANANE
Musa paradisiaca *(Musaceas)*

IMP RICHIER-LAUGIER-PARIS   Musée scolaire — LES FILS D'ÉMILE DEYROLLE, 46, rue du Bac, Paris (7ᵉ)

Fruit
(exotic)

Botanical plate no. 48 B
Late nineteenth–
early twentieth century
"Deyrolle Educational Museum"
Éditions Les Fils d'Émile Deyrolle
46 rue du Bac, 7th arr., Paris
Imprimerie Richier Laugier

The pineapple was the king of fruits at the eighteenth-century French court. In this plate from Émile Deyrolle's "educational museum" (*musée scolaire*), it has been placed on a pedestal. Originally from Central America and Brazil—introduced at the time of Charles V, then enjoyed by Louis XIV—pineapples were one of the first exotic pleasures to be consumed in Europe. Louis XV even had them grown in his royal greenhouses, which were kept heated after the frosts of early November.

The plate makes use of color shading, as can be seen in the dissolving of the green of the avocado and guava into the yellow of the banana and lemon. Apart from the last fruit of the list—which is mentioned in the writings of Aristophanes, but was little liked in antiquity—they all had to await the discovery of the American continent before they could grace Europe's most luxurious tables. These exotic fruits long remained exceptional foodstuffs, with proven virtues.

The lemon, which was imported by the Arabs during the Crusades, was, during the eighteenth century, a state secret that the British navy—and Captain James Cook in particular—took care not to reveal to the French fleets. With cargoes of lemons aboard, the sailors avoided catching scurvy.

Guava is a Brazilian fruit that tastes like peaches and strawberries. Just 3½ oz. (100 g) is enough to cover our daily vitamin C requirements. Its highly juicy, fresh pulp is packed with little seeds, like a tomato.

As for the avocado—the fruit of a tree from South America—its smooth, fatty flesh takes on a flavor of pistachios and fresh butter. It is a delicacy suited to both sweet and savory uses.

And finally, bananas—those blond beauties that turn brown over time. This plant from the West and East Indies was imported into France as early as the nineteenth century. Josephine Baker contributed magnificently to their renown, by sporting them so gracefully in her iconic banana skirt.

FRUITS

ABRICOTIER
ABRICOTS
Prunus armeniaca (Rosacées)

ORANGER
ORANGE
Citrus aurantium (hespéridées)

CITRONNIER
CITRON ou LIMON
Citrus limon (hespéridées)

PRUNIER
PRUNE REINE-CLAUDE
Prunus insititia (Rosacées)

AMANDIER
AMANDES
Amygdalus communis (Rosacées)

VIGNE
RAISIN BLANC
Vitis vinifera (Ampélidées)

NOYER
NOIX
Juglans regia (Juglandées)

POIRIER
POIRE
Pirus communis (Rosacées)

IMP RICHIER·LAUGIER·PARIS

Musée scolaire. — LES FILS D'ÉMILE DEYROLLE, 46, Rue du Bac, Paris (7e)

Fruit

(fruit trees)

Botanical plate no. 49 A

**Late nineteenth–
early twentieth century**

"Deyrolle Educational Museum"
Éditions Les Fils d'Émile Deyrolle
46 rue du Bac, 7th arr., Paris
Imprimerie Richier Laugier

Raw, cooked, or dried fruits have been nourishing mankind since prehistory. Some are acidic and refreshing, like oranges and lemons. Others are sweet and eloquently herald the arrival of summer, like apricots, plums, or green almonds. Then grapes announce the coming of fall, before pears and nuts take us into winter. No need for schoolchildren to get out their calendars: thanks to Émile Deyrolle, the cycle of fruits is expressed in the delicacy and precision of this drawing.

This plate from the "educational museum" (*musée scolaire*) is focused on various species. While the names of the fruits are clearly mentioned, they only come after the names of their trees. Alongside the roundness of the Reine-Claude plums (the name of King Francis I's first wife) or the wonderfully bunched-up, pearl-like white grapes (the original seedlings of which were supposedly sown by Noah), the educational purpose of this plate can be seen in the depiction of the foliage and the smooth or rough grain of the branches. Walnut, lemon, and pear trees may have distinct cell lines, but they all find favor with cabinetmakers.

Yet this composition must also have made curious children's mouths water. Oranges were not part of working-class diets until the 1950s, so the children were unlikely to know what they tasted like. On the other hand, they would have been familiar with plums, pears, and grapes with their small ticklish seeds. But did they know that the seeds of the almond tree are edible, which is not the case for all fruit trees? Indeed, care must be taken with apricots, which conceal in their midst a delightful kernel full of prussic acid, a deadly poison.

FRUITS

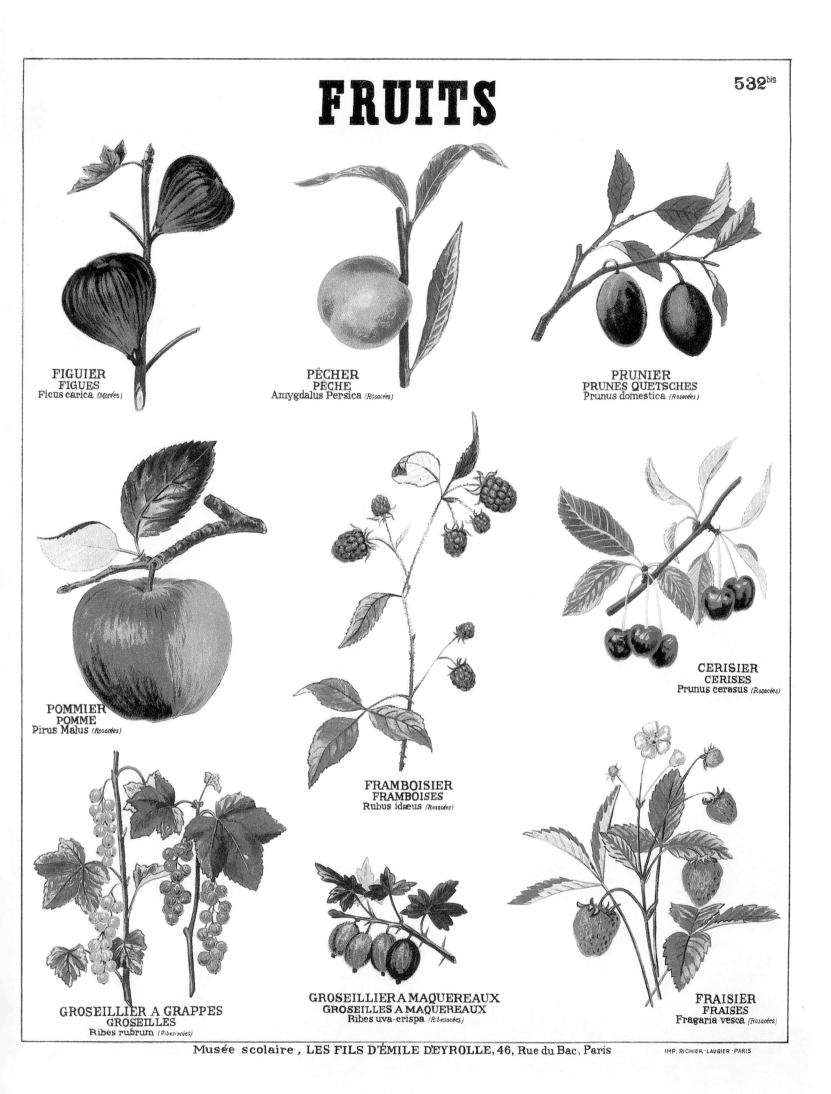

FIGUIER
FIGUES
Ficus carica *(Morées)*

PÊCHER
PÊCHE
Amygdalus Persica *(Rosacées)*

PRUNIER
PRUNES QUETSCHES
Prunus domestica *(Rosacées)*

POMMIER
POMME
Pirus Malus *(Rosacées)*

CERISIER
CERISES
Prunus cerasus *(Rosacées)*

FRAMBOISIER
FRAMBOISES
Rubus idæus *(Rosacées)*

GROSEILLIER A GRAPPES
GROSEILLES
Ribes rubrum *(Ribesiacées)*

GROSEILLIER A MAQUEREAUX
GROSEILLES A MAQUEREAUX
Ribes uva-crispa *(Ribesiacées)*

FRAISIER
FRAISES
Fragaria vesca *(Rosacées)*

Musée scolaire, LES FILS D'ÉMILE D'EYROLLE, 46, Rue du Bac, Paris   IMP. RICHIER·LAUGIER·PARIS

Fruit
(red)

Botanical plate no. 532bis
Late nineteenth–
early twentieth century
"Deyrolle Educational Museum"
Éditions Les Fils d'Émile Deyrolle
46 rue du Bac, 7th arr., Paris
Imprimerie Richier Laugier

In his treatise on color, the writer Antoine Furetière (1619–1688) pointed out that the gleaming look of red might embody fire. He even revealed a secret of master glassmakers, who added a few drops of gold so as to produce a sparkle like a ruby.

The palette of varieties that are depicted here—commonly called "red fruit"—still hold this privileged position. Apples attain it spontaneously, along with a hint of yellow, while peaches lean more toward orange, and figs and damsons can claim to be "red" thanks to their almost black-mauve color. They all taste of summer—which they herald, as strawberries do, or bring to a close, like apples—while exuding a scent of warm, relaxing days.

The fig is one of the fruits depicted on Egyptian murals. While apples are well known thanks to the story of Adam and Eve, it was a broad, green fig leaf that seems to have covered their nudity. It is an emblematic Mediterranean fruit, as delicious dried as it is fresh. The heritage of the raspberry is no less prestigious. Greek mythology relates how Zeus, when still a child, was in such a fit of anger that his nurse—the nymph Ida—calmed him down by giving him a raspberry. It was by pricking her breast with one of them that Ida permanently changed the color of this fruit, which used to be white, with her blood.

Each fruit has its own history and distinct list of appeals. Peaches, originally from Persia, are particularly appreciated for their flesh, concealed beneath a slightly tart, velvety skin. Gooseberries have a refreshing acidity that erupts from them. As for cherries, starlings are just as partial as humans to these small, long-stemmed fruits, the stems of which are also used to make infusions with diuretic properties.

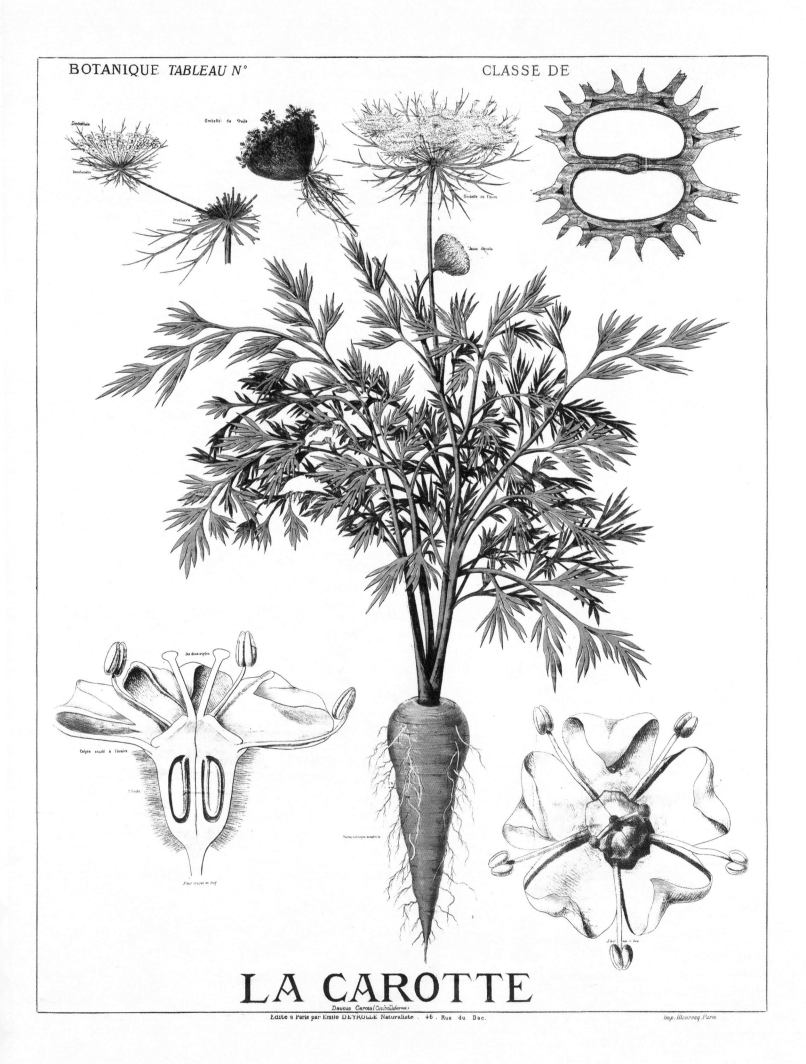

LA CAROTTE

Daucus Carota (Ombellifères)

Edité à Paris par Emile DEYROLLE Naturaliste . 46 . Rue du Bac.   Imp. Monrocq, Paris

The Carrot
Daucus carota
(Umbellifers)

Botanical plate
Late nineteenth– early twentieth century
Éditions Émile Deyrolle
46 rue du Bac, 7th arr., Paris
Imprimerie Gaillac-Monrocq & Cie

The carrot, *Daucus carota*, with its tip pointing toward the "O" in its name and its main flower reaching upward, is thriving in the center of this plate. In this graphic depiction, all of the elements of this root plant can be seen.

The carrot first stands out by contrast: from the deep green of its finely crafted foliage to the delightful orange of its chubby root and the pointillist whiteness of its sprigs of fresh flowers. Ignoring any timelines, the educational designer commissioned by Émile Deyrolle also set about depicting a dry stalk on either side of the central umbel, which will later spread the pointed seeds that are contained in an envelope divided into two lobes.

In the capitulary *De villis*, Charlemagne provided exemplarily precise instructions about the roots that should be cultivated and the fruit trees or flowers that should be grown in his lands. The carrot is one of the ninety species that ought to be present in every monastery or imperial garden. But both its look and taste were quite different from the sweet tenderness that we are used to today. Imagine a scrawnier, woodier plant, bitter to the taste and whitish, like its wild cousin, to which it is still very close. The carrots served to this emperor of the Middle Ages had their imperfections concealed beneath a slice of mutton.

During the eighteenth century, this root vegetable began to be actively cultivated, having turned orange following a mutation that occurred in Holland. After improvements over the centuries, carrots no longer have a fibrous core, but still remain rich in precious vitamin A. This vitamin—which is indispensable to the workings of the immune system—improves the eyesight, as well as the beauty of the skin and health of the mucous membranes. Other (alleged) examples of its virtues include turning thighs pink and restoring amiability.

LE FRAISIER

Fragaria Vesca (Rosacées)

Edité à Paris par Emile DEYROLLE, Naturaliste, 23, rue de la Monnaie

The Strawberry Plant
Fragaria vesca
(Rose Family)

Botanical plate
Second half
of the nineteenth century

Éditions Émile Deyrolle
23 rue de la Monnaie, 1st arr., Paris
Imprimerie Gaillac-Monrocq & Cie

Everything about this Émile Deyrolle plate is delicate. *Fragaria vesca*—the wild strawberry—is an uncultivated variety that is known to have been eaten since the Middle Ages. Seemingly dancing on the page while escaping from their maternal stem, the creeping stems (or stolons) are decked with leaves, having three soft green, indented leaflets. This natural beauty blossoms in springtime. Its five round petals—whose stamens are gilded and white—are edible. However, that would mean forgoing the small, intensely fragrant, tartly flavored red fruits that emerge from them.

In the grand food chain, which sees trees bear fruits and herbaceous plants turn into vegetables, strawberries are an exception as they come from a perennial. In terms of vitamin C, they surpass oranges but are outdistanced by blackcurrants and parsley. The great names of the Enlightenment—such as the Swedish naturalist Carl Linnaeus or the writer and scientist Fontenelle, who died at a ripe old age—praised their medicinal properties.

At the end of the reign of Louis XIV, a French officer with a predestined surname, Amédée-François Frézier (pronounced just like *fraisier*, the French word for strawberry plant), brought back from Chile five seedlings of an indigenous strawberry, which was incredibly white and far fleshier than the small variety that grew by roadsides. After several mutations that turned it red, this is the variety that continues to exist in most contemporary strawberries.

PLANTES
FRUITS ET GRAINES

Le fruit résulte de la transformation d'une partie de la fleur.
La graine est la partie essentielle du fruit; elle est composée d'une enveloppe qui renferme la plantule qui possède une racine, une tige avec 1, 2 ou plusieurs cotylédons; quand la graine germe, cette plantule, en se développant, devient la plante.

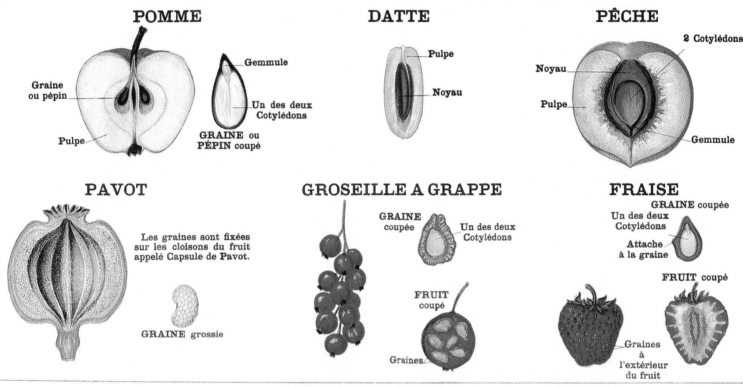

POMME
Gemmule — Graine ou pépin — Un des deux Cotylédons — Pulpe — GRAINE ou PÉPIN coupé

DATTE
Pulpe — Noyau

PÊCHE
2 Cotylédons — Noyau — Pulpe — Gemmule

PAVOT
Les graines sont fixées sur les cloisons du fruit appelé Capsule de Pavot.
GRAINE grossie

GROSEILLE A GRAPPE
GRAINE coupée — Un des deux Cotylédons — FRUIT coupé — Graines

FRAISE
GRAINE coupée — Un des deux Cotylédons — Attache à la graine — FRUIT coupé — Graines à l'extérieur du fruit

GERMINATION

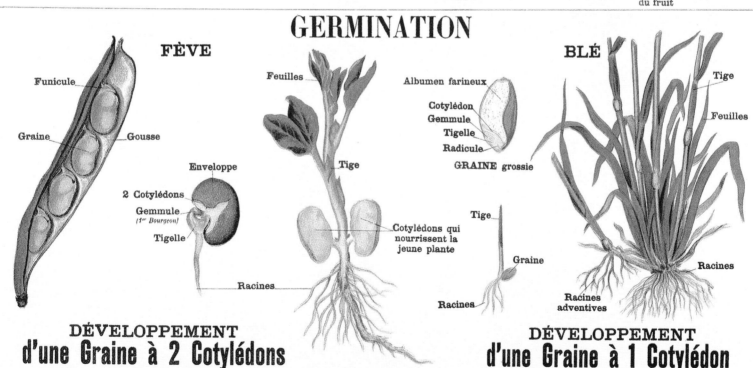

FÈVE
Funicule — Graine — Gousse — Enveloppe — 2 Cotylédons — Gemmule (1ᵉʳ Bourgeon) — Tigelle

Feuilles — Tige — Cotylédons qui nourrissent la jeune plante — Racines

BLÉ
Albumen farineux — Cotylédon — Gemmule — Tigelle — Radicule — GRAINE grossie

Tige — Feuilles — Tige — Graine — Racines — Racines adventives

DÉVELOPPEMENT
d'une Graine à 2 Cotylédons

DÉVELOPPEMENT
d'une Graine à 1 Cotylédon

La germination est le développement de la graine en plante.
Les Cotylédons constituent les premières feuilles de la plantule; souvent ils contiennent des réserves qui servent de première nourriture à la plante.

IMP. RICHIER-LAUGIER. Mobilier et Matériel pour l'Enseignement. — Établissements DEYROLLE, 46, Rue du Bac, Paris-7ᵉ

Plants
—
Fruits and Seeds
—
Germination

Botanical plate no. 10
Late nineteenth–
early twentieth century
"Teaching Supplies and Material"
Établissements Deyrolle, Éditeurs
46 rue du Bac, 7th arr., Paris
Imprimerie Richier Laugier

This plate has been divided in two: the top half features a study of fruits derived from the corresponding seeds; the bottom half shows the principle of germination. No matter how many straight lines are used in Deyrolle's "teaching supplies and material," it is nevertheless a circular shape that instantly springs to mind: it is, after all, the cycle of life that is being explained here. Since the invention of agriculture, mankind has understood the principle of seed germination and the reproduction of plants. We have long realized that by placing in the earth a seed—which itself is a fruit born of the transformation of a flower— we would hopefully reproduce the species.

Plants are living beings that are immobile, but which derive their nourishment from the earth, air, and water. Step by step and with a light gracefulness, this plate takes us behind the scenes to reveal their private life. We see, as though from behind a theater curtain, what is generally hidden from our eyes. The fruits are cut in half and the seed itself reveals its hidden side, with the various organs that constitute it. One of the greatest strengths of plants resides in their ability to show no signs of life. A bean or pea seed, or a potato harvested in the fall remain alive. This is proved in springtime, when the cycle of reproduction tells them to wake up. They then set about germinating and, if put back into the soil, they will give rise to new specimens.

That is the very principle of this marvelously educative plate. It is a lesson that proceeds gently, allowing us to easily understand what makes up the essence of plant life: a root stuck in the earth, a stalk to search for light, and leaves to bear fruit. This has been an uninterrupted, magical cycle for millions of years, as beautiful and simple as that of a human life.

PLANTES
DICOTYLÉDONES (GRAINES A 2 COTYLÉDONS)

FAMILLE DES OLÉACÉES

Comprend comme genre principal l'Olivier dont le fruit sert à faire de l'huile.

OLIVIER

Fruit ou drupe appelé olive

Péricarpe

Noyau

FRUIT COUPÉ

Pistil

Étamines

4 pétales soudés à la base

FLEUR grossie

Les OLÉACÉES ont 2 étamines. Le pistil se compose de 2 carpelles soudés en un ovaire à 2 loges.

FAMILLE DES ROSACÉES

Comprend la plupart de nos arbres fruitiers (Poirier, Prunier, Pêcher, Cognassier, Néflier), les Framboisiers, Fraisiers, Rosiers.

POMMIER

Étamines nombreuses

Corolle à 5 pétales insérés sur le calice

Pistil

Calice à 5 sépales

Ovaire

FLEUR COUPÉE (grossie)

Les ROSACÉES ont la corolle de 5 pétales égaux disposés en rosaces, les étamines nombreuses fixées sur le calice.

FAMILLE DES CRUCIFÈRES

Cresson, Moutarde, Chou, Navet, Radis, Giroflée.

COLZA

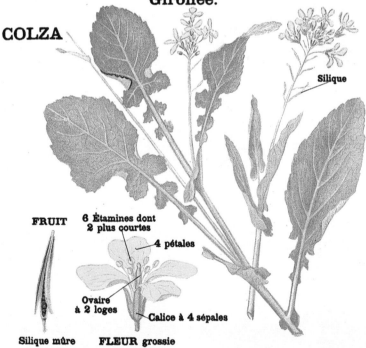

Silique

FRUIT

6 Étamines dont 2 plus courtes

4 pétales

Ovaire à 2 loges

Calice à 4 sépales

Silique mûre

FLEUR grossie

Les CRUCIFÈRES ont les fleurs à 4 pétales réguliers en forme de croix, 6 étamines, le fruit est une silique à 2 loges.

FAMILLE DES AMPÉLIDÉES

Comprend la Vigne dont le fruit est le raisin

VIGNE

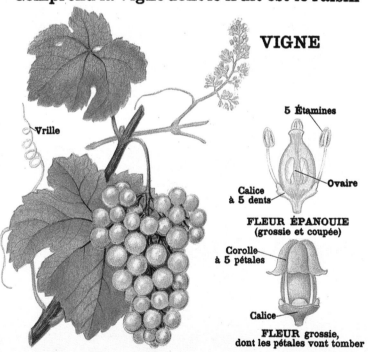

Vrille

5 Étamines

Ovaire

Calice à 5 dents

FLEUR ÉPANOUIE (grossie et coupée)

Corolle à 5 pétales

Calice

FLEUR grossie, dont les pétales vont tomber

Les AMPÉLIDÉES ont la tige grimpante garnie de vrilles, les fleurs vertes, petites, à 5 pétales soudés en haut, 5 étamines. La corolle tombe quand la fleur s'épanouit.

Plants
—
Dicotyledons
(Seeds with Two Cotyledons)

Botanical plate no. 14
Late nineteenth–
early twentieth century
"Teaching Supplies and Material"
Établissements Deyrolle, Éditeurs
46 rue du Bac, 7th arr., Paris
Imprimerie Richier Laugier

Divided into four equal boxes, the species depicted here seem to be playing at Happy Families. "In the cruciferous family, I want the mother," a child might say, mingling a desire to learn with the pleasure of a game. So, each member's role would need to be determined.

What among the cabbages, turnips, radishes, cress, mustard, wallflowers, or rape could embody the various generations? They are all born from flowers with four petals, arranged in a cross, a geometric form to which they owe their name: cruciferous. Their prickly leaves can be found just as readily on rocky mountain paths, dune hillocks, damp embankments, or dry lawns.

The next box, in the bottom right-hand corner, highlights a fine bunch of white grapes with fleshy seeds. While the fruits have always been the most coveted part of the vine (birds devour them, too), in Greece, the leaves are eaten stuffed and sprinkled with olive oil. The tendril, spiraled like a corkscrew, is a little coil that allows this rambling shrub to stand erect. But whether the grapes are black, red, or an almost golden yellow, once pressed they produce a similar transparent juice. It is then up to the winegrowers to adapt the maceration of the skins to obtain the desired intensity of crimson.

The olive family can be seen in the top left-hand corner: 11 lb. (5 kg) of its fruits will provide a little over a pint of oil. And finally, the rose family—fruit trees and shrubs with varied destinies, from a three-hundred-year-old pear tree to the formidable thorns of the bramble.

Beyond a study of the characteristics of each of these families, there is another way to interpret this plate. On the same table can be seen vegetables and fruits, oil and wine. A simplicity with an exemplary dietary balance, making marvelous combinations of tastes and colors possible. A delicious perspective.

PLANTES AROMATIQUES

CANNELLE (Laurus cinnamomum)

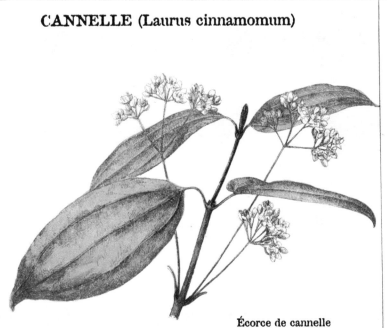

Écorce de cannelle

GIROFLIER (Caryophyllus aromaticus)

Nombreuses étamines

5 pétales

Clou de girofle

VANILLE (Vanilla aromatica)

Gousse

POIVRIER (Piper nigrum)

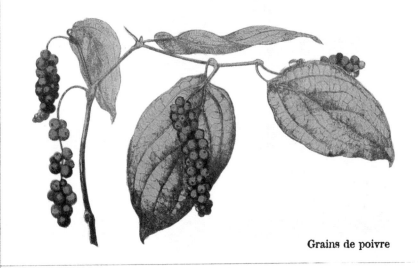

Grains de poivre

MUSCADIER (Myristica fragans)

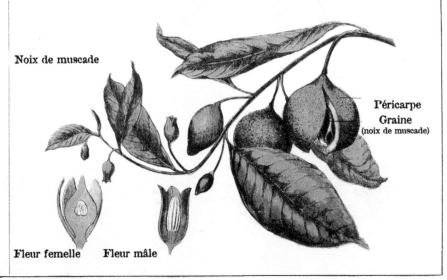

Noix de muscade

Péricarpe
Graine
(noix de muscade)

Fleur femelle   Fleur mâle

EMILE DEYROLLE   46, RUE DU BAC. PARIS

Aromatic Plants

Botanical plate no. 43 A
Late nineteenth–
early twentieth century
Éditions Émile Deyrolle
46 rue du Bac, 7th arr., Paris

"As expensive as pepper." This was still a commonplace expression during the age of the Enlightenment; Voltaire used it in his writings. It highlights, indirectly, the importance of the spice trade and the battles waged over the centuries by navigators from around the world—from Vasco da Gama to the Dutch navy—to keep a monopoly on it.

Aromatics were a new form of gold—with bewitching fragrances—yet they had ancient usages. Owning them was a sign of wealth. The aristocrats of the Middle Ages used them abundantly to smother their over-mature meat, or else to enhance their desserts and wines. Cinnamon was doubtless the first in a long series of spices that followed the Silk Road to Europe. Originally from the island of Ceylon (now Sri Lanka), this bark, tinged with a brown, almost red color, can be savored once it has been reduced to a powder. Its warm, scented flavor can also be found in its leaves, which are used in infusions.

Brought together here in a single plate, clove, vanilla, pepper, nutmeg, and cinnamon plants each embody in their own way an exoticism that the West has now made its own. If mapped out in culinary terms, they could appear in the same recipe for gingerbread.

As regards pepper, the little black, white or red corns, all from the same tree, are well known. We forget, though, that it is a creeper, the growth of which needs to be controlled. Cloves—which Indonesians mix with their tobacco—are in fact the plant's buds, darkened by the sun. What is commonly called "nutmeg"—which the painter Toulouse-Lautrec grated into his port wine—is the kernel of a fruit wrapped up in bright red filaments, or mace, which is another spicy treasure. Finally, the tender and finely scented vanilla arrived in Spain in the sixteenth century, at the same time as cacao. With its proud, graceful lines, this exotic plant from the orchid family produces a dark pod, which needs to be left to rest for several months before its cortex is titillated with the tip of a knife.

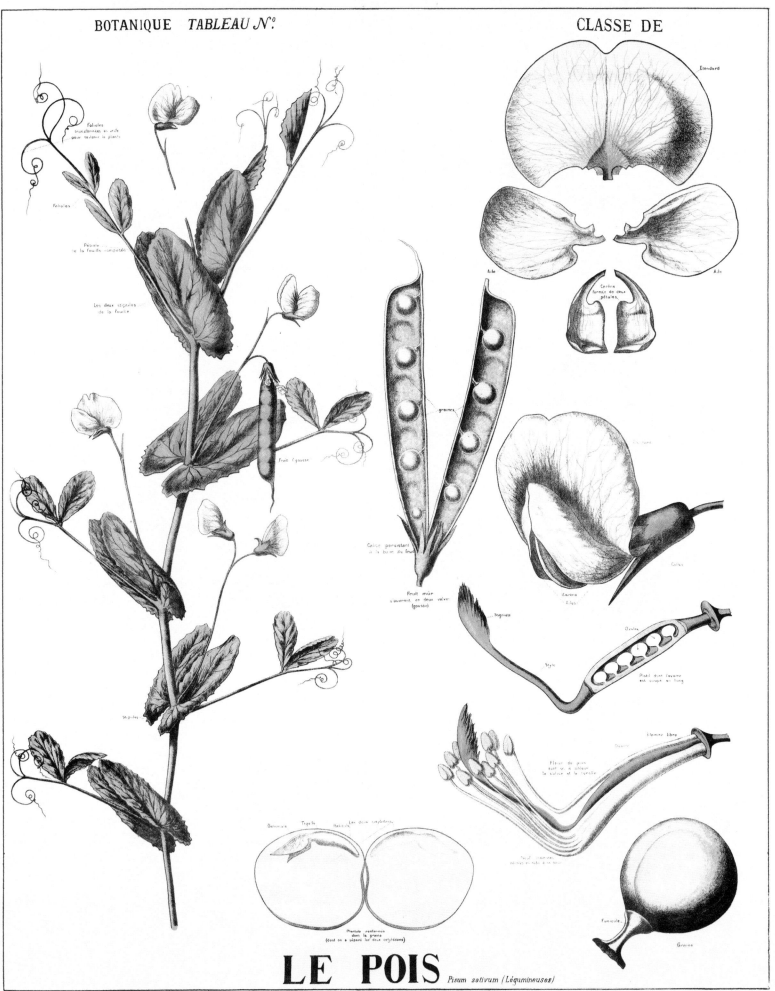

LE POIS

Pisum sativum (Légumineuses)

Edité à Paris par Emile DEYROLLE, Naturaliste, 23, Rue de la Monnaie.

The Pea
Pisum sativum
(Legume Family)

Botanical plate
Second half
of the nineteenth century
Éditions Émile Deyrolle
23 rue de la Monnaie, 1st arr., Paris
Imprimerie Gaillac-Monrocq & Cie

Louis XIV was partial to them. He ate them so avidly each spring that this little green vegetable, tender and filled with sweet water, reduced Fagon—the monarch's first doctor—to despair. In his record of the king's health, the *Journal de la santé du roi Louis XIV*, he mentions on several occasions fits of dizziness that afflicted his majesty: "They occurred especially on those days when his stomach never emptied," he wrote. "But above all during the season when the king filled his belly at every meal with a huge quantity of peas." This taste for pulses, eaten fresh, was new, and these stars of the royal kitchen garden were rapidly adopted by the court, the better to please the sovereign. "This business of the peas is still continuing," Madame de Maintenon, the king's secret wife, wrote in 1696. "His impatience before eating them, his pleasure after eating them, and his joy in eating even more are the three points that our Princes have been coping with these past four days. There are women who, after supping—and supping well—with the King, find peas at home to eat before going to bed, at the risk of contracting indigestion. It is a fashion, a rage, and one leads to the other."

Like cereals, they were recognized for their nutritional value, and at the time were eaten dried—a far cry from the famous recipe of the old royal Abbey of Fontevraud, as described by Alexandre Dumas in his great culinary dictionary, which combined these small green spheres with lettuce heart, butter, cream, egg yolk, and a small spoonful of sugar.

But what attracts the eye on this educational plate are the meticulous, complex details featured. As an annual plant (which needs to be sown again each year), its frail stalk would be incapable of remaining upright if it had not evolved elaborate tendrils that cling onto the stakes provided by gardeners. After being carefully stripped of leaves, the upper section of *Pisum sativum* reveals a large standard petal, two wing petals, and finally a trough—called a calyx—in which the stamen and pistil develop. The latter provides the fruit, enclosed inside a pod whose two halves can be separated to liberate the seeds, which are then ready for any gourmet's palate.

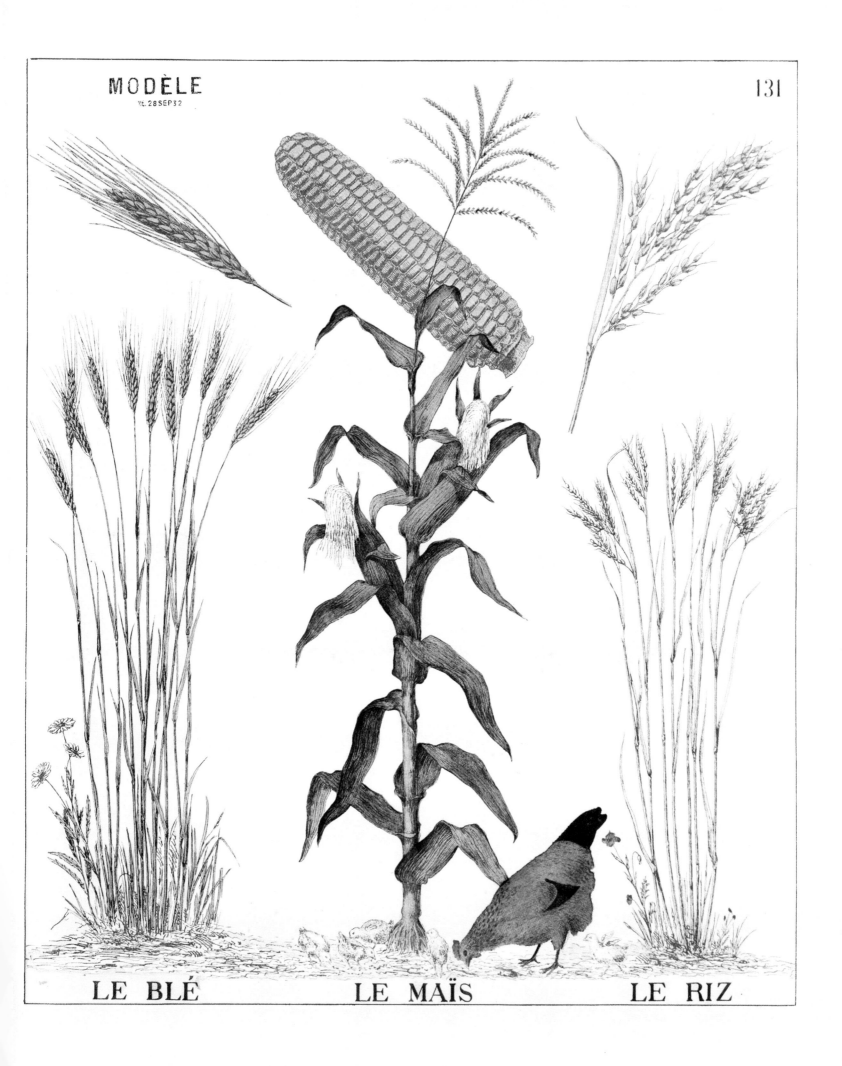

LE BLÉ   LE MAÏS   LE RIZ

Wheat, Maize, and Rice

Botanical plate no. 131
Late nineteenth–early twentieth century

Here come the high grasses. As part of a cosmopolitan family of 12,000 species, they have been able to adapt to all climates and thrive at every latitude. Whether in rice paddies, on the steppes, or in prairies, they now occupy about 70 percent of the world's arable land. While being essential to a balanced human diet, grasses also provide nourishment for other animals, as can be seen in this poetic Deyrolle plate, in which a little red hen and her chicks are feeding on seeds that have fallen to the ground.

"Both urban and rural gleaners bend over, the better to gather," remarked the filmmaker Agnès Varda in the documentary she devoted to this ancestral gesture, also immortalized by Jean-François Millet in 1857 in his painting *The Gleaners*: three clearly impoverished peasant women are bending over to pick up the ears of wheat left behind after the harvest. This treasure will make a welcome addition to their meals.

Owing to their nutritional wealth, grasses can be credited with the development of various civilizations, three of which are represented here: rice in Asia, maize (or corn) in America, and wheat in the Mediterranean basin. All that is missing is millet, which originated on the African continent.

Set majestically in the center of the drawing, the maize plant—which was a gift from the New World and no doubt arrived in Europe thanks to Christopher Columbus—stands out from its fellows thanks to its flowers, which separate the stamens on one side from the pistils on the other. As on a small palm tree, the stamens are found at the top of the stalk, while the pistils—the future fleshy ears containing multiple seeds—can be found on its sides. Rice is a lover of damp, marshy land and, just like wheat or maize, can be made into flour. A certain idea of universality thus emerges from this educational image: freed from all notions of borders or cultures, mankind has been sharing its love of bread for thousands of years, from one side of the world to the other.

Glumelle inférieure

Stigmates plumeux

Etamine

Etamine

Pistil

Etamine

Fleur dont on a enlevé
la glumelle supérieure

Epi de fleurs

Feuilles à nervures
longitudinales

Chaume

Epillet

Epi dépillets

Feuille à nervures
parallèles

Chaume

Liguie

Gaine fendue

Axe de l'épi

Stigmates plumeux

Etamines

Enveloppes de la graine
et du fruit soudés
en un seul tégument

Glume inférieure

Glume supérieure

Albumen

Cotyledon

Plumule

Racines adventives

Radicule

Fruit coupé

Epillet
de fleurs

LE BLÉ

Triticum Vulgare Graminées)

Edité à Paris par Emile **DEYROLLE** Naturaliste, 2 3, Rue de la Monnaie

Wheat
Triticum vulgare
(Grasses)

Botanical plate
Second half
of the nineteenth century
Éditions Émile Deyrolle
23 rue de la Monnaie, 1st arr., Paris

About 10,000 years BCE, during the Neolithic era, prehistoric men discovered the principle of turning wheat into bread, with or without the use of yeast. *Triticum vulgare*—a cereal from the grass family—is unusual in that its seeds contain starch: thanks to a fermentation reaction with yeast, carbon dioxide is given off, which makes the bread rise.

After growing in a wild state in the Middle East, wheat was then cultivated in the Near East, before reaching Europe. In Greek and Roman antiquity it became, along with olives and vines, an embodiment of the simple life, in harmony with the earth.

In this mostly green plate, the legendary blond color of wheat is still nascent. The focus is instead on its flowering. Linked together in a perfectly parallel pattern on either side of the stalk's axis, the groups of flowers hint at the gold lurking beneath them. A short peduncle connects them to the branch. However, the leaves are long, narrow, and folded almost in half. The famous medieval household management book *Le Ménagier de Paris* (1393) provides a recipe for verjuice—an acidic preparation that can replace vinegar—which is made from the plant's leaves.

When wheat reaches maturity, the seeds are removed from the ears. They are then ground into flour, so that the seed coat can break down into the yellow flakes known as "bran." Wheat also has "false friends": buckwheat or "black wheat" (*Polygonum fagopyrum*) is one of them, but the two are totally dissimilar. In the same way, distinctions should be made between "hard" and "soft" wheat. In France, only soft wheat was grown until World War I; hard wheat—an essential ingredient of pasta—arrived later. It is richer in gluten but poorer in starch.

Wheat is also the principal ingredient of couscous, which has enjoyed widespread popularity in France since the 1960s. However, François Rabelais served it four centuries earlier to Gargantua in his *Pantagruel* (1532), as *coscosson* doused with broth.

PLANTES
DICOTYLÉDONES (GRAINES A 2 COTYLÉDONS)

FAMILLE DES OMBELLIFÈRES

Panais, Cerfeuil, Persil, Céleri, Angélique.
Ciguë (poison violent).

5 étamines
5 Stigmates
5 Pétales
CAROTTE
Ovaire à 2 loges et à 2 ovules
Calice soudé au pistil sur la longueur de l'ovaire
Fleur coupée au milieu grossie
FRUIT
Racine pivotante

FAMILLE DES SOLANÉES

Usuelles : Aubergine, Tabac, Tomate.
Vénéneuses : Belladone, Morelle, Pomme épineuse.

POMME DE TERRE

Stigmate
Corolle à 5 pétales soudés
5 étamines
Style
Ovaire à 2 loges
Calice non soudé à l'ovaire
Fleur coupée au milieu grossie
FRUIT grossi
Tubercules

Les **OMBELLIFÈRES** ont 5 pétales et 5 étamines. Les fleurs sont petites, nombreuses, réunies au sommet de la tige en forme d'ombrelle, appelée ombelle.

Les **SOLANÉES** ont la corolle à 5 pétales avec 5 étamines ; le fruit renferme beaucoup de graines.

IMP. INCKER - LAUGER-PARIS - 734-70-08   Mobilier et Matériel pour l'Enseignement. — Établissements DEYROLLE, 46, Rue du Bac, Paris-7°

Plants
—
Dicotyledons
(Seeds with Two Cotyledons)

Botanical plate no. 11
Late nineteenth–
early twentieth century
"Teaching Supplies and Material"
Établissements Deyrolle, Éditeurs
46 rue du Bac, 7th arr., Paris
Imprimerie Richier Laugier

The umbellifers and nightshades appear perfectly symmetrical. The carrot and the potato represent a selection of their most reputed members. As in a mirror image, the orange roots of one face the yellow tubers of the other, while the five-petalled flowers, sprouting from an intensely green foliage, venture toward the sky. Brought together under the umbrella term "dicotyledonous plants" (that is to say, an embryo with two lobes, and two leaves coming out of the seed), the carrot and potato seem to be evenly matched.

However, historically the latter had difficulties being accepted into French cuisine. It long remained disliked and misunderstood, before becoming indispensable during times of crisis or famine. It was discovered in Peru by the Spanish, who brought it to Europe in the sixteenth century, but people did not know how to eat it and it often ended up being grilled like a chestnut and eaten with its skin. It was a pharmacist—Antoine Augustin Parmentier—who cunningly persuaded Louis XVI to develop its cultivation and turn it into an object of desire. During a festival, he suggested to the king that he wear a potato blossom in his buttonhole, before having this tuber served in splendid style at the banquet. Finally, he had potatoes planted in the king's gardens, watched over by the army, but that did not prevent the local market-gardeners from pilfering them— a roundabout way of popularizing these plants.

Yet Deyrolle's plate goes further than this. It is a warning against poisonous cousins and toxic parents, because the family tree of the umbellifers and nightshades includes strange members that do need to be treated with caution. The famous hemlock that killed Socrates shares characteristics with wild carrots. As for belladonna, which—like the eggplant—comes from the same family as the potato, it possesses a deceptive beauty: eating a dozen of its little dark berries is lethal for humans.

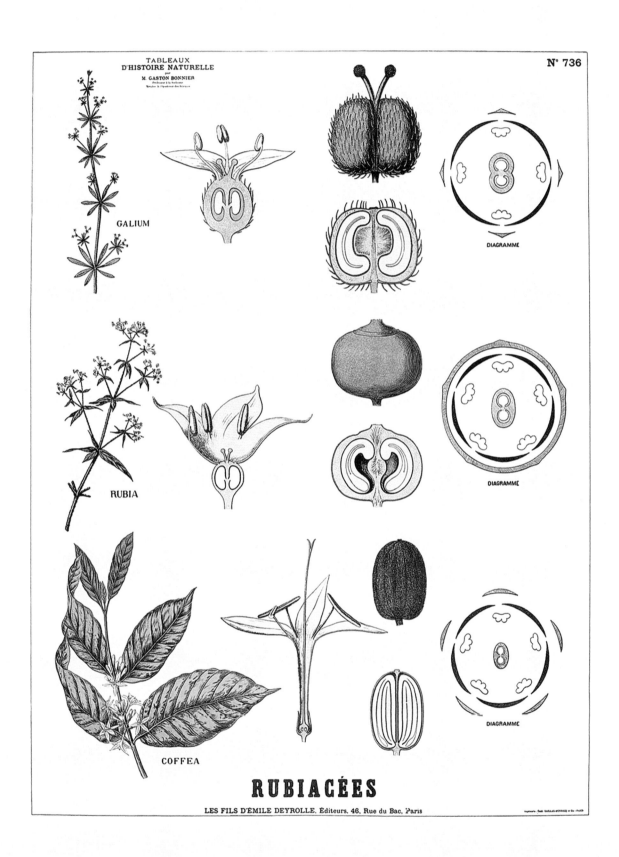

TABLEAUX
D'HISTOIRE NATURELLE
par
M. GASTON BONNIER

GALIUM

DIAGRAMME

RUBIA

DIAGRAMME

COFFEA

DIAGRAMME

RUBIACÉES

LES FILS D'ÉMILE DEYROLLE, Éditeurs, 46, Rue du Bac, Paris

Rubiaceae
(Madder Family)

Natural history plate no. 736
Late nineteenth– early twentieth century

By Gaston Bonnier,
professor at the Sorbonne and member
of the Académie des Sciences
Éditions Les Fils d'Émile Deyrolle
46 rue du Bac, 7th arr., Paris
Imprimerie Gaillac-Monrocq & Cie

What an attractive plate! And not just thanks to its graceful composition, in which each stalk, flower, and seed stands out from the white page. The attraction is quite literal—this is one of the whimsical aspects of *Galium aparine*, which Émile Deyrolle's sons, pursuing their father's educational work, have depicted in the top left-hand corner. This plant is commonly called "cleavers" or "goosegrass," and we have all returned from a casual stroll in a field with its hairy, perfectly round, and slightly prickly fruits attached firmly to our pant legs.

The central plant—*Rubia tinctorum*—gives its name to the family which is depicted here: the Rubiaceae. While they do not grow in all parts of the world, they all have these characteristically round fruits. Grown in the South of France for the dye that is extracted from its roots, *Rubia* is known in French as *garance* ("madder" in English). This became a tragically elegant color, because it was adopted by the French army for the pants of its troops' uniforms, only to be replaced by a sky blue in 1916 so as to avoid—or a little more so—the enemy's bullets.

To conclude this trilogy, there is coffee, or *Coffea arabica*. While this floral diagram displays a clear botanical kinship, its broader leaves have fragrant white flowers. But its renown comes from its seeds. Originally from Yemen, coffee was already known to the Egyptians. It reached France in the mid-seventeenth century, and Louis XIV had it planted in his château at Marly, even though this small roasted bean with its aromatic nature needed warmer climes to flourish. There was such a trend for coffee that, in Constantinople, imams complained about mosques being empty as friends preferred to take a coffee break together. Johann Sebastian Bach even dedicated a cantata to it—BWV 211, or the "Coffee Cantata"— the musical tale of a father worried about the consumption of this dark drink, which his young daughter would not have traded for a thousand kisses.

GÉOGRAPHIE ÉCONOMIQUE ET AGRICOLE
ALIMENTATION - LES ARBRES FRUITIERS

Par Albert BERNARD
Instituteur
Officier de l'Instruction Publique

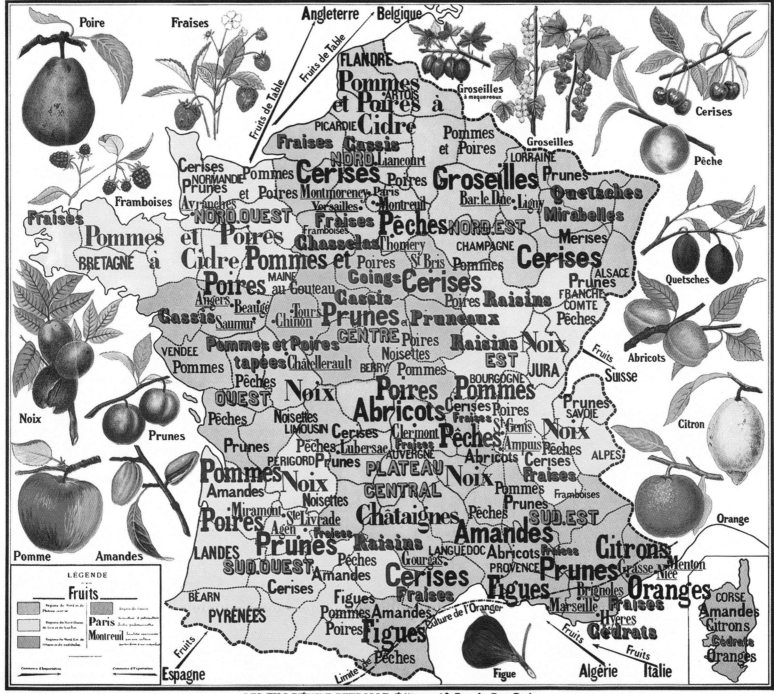

LES FILS D'ÉMILE DEYROLLE, Éditeurs, 46, Rue du Bac, Paris

Food
—
◆
Fruit Trees

Agricultural map no. 6
Late nineteenth–
early twentieth century

"Economic and Agricultural Geography"
by Albert Bernard, schoolmaster
and public education officer
Éditions Les Fils d'Émile Deyrolle
46 rue du Bac, 7th arr., Paris
Imprimerie Gaillac-Monrocq & Cie

Apples, pears, peaches, and apricots appear in a well-known French nursery rhyme from Saint-Bueil, a small village in the Isère department in eastern France. It is a song that the pupils of Albert Bernard, the creator of this agricultural map of fruit trees, must have sung in unison. It is interesting to note that this plate by Deyrolle clearly confirms the presence of these four species in the east-central region of France. It also displays the production of walnuts in this region, which extended the reputation of the town of Grenoble far beyond the French borders. Concerned about the quality of the produce being sold, in 1938 the producers established the first "appellation d'origine contrôlée" (AOC) applied to a fruit. This successful trade had begun a century earlier thanks to flourishing exports to the west coast of the United States.

There can be no doubt that the image is bright and colorful, fresh and delightful. As with all cartography, it provides an opportunity for daydreaming as well as learning. There is no need to have a fertile imagination to feel the velvety caress of peaches or smell the invigorating scent of lemon peel, those renowned products from the town of Menton. And, while the plate's beauty lies in the incredible richness of the varieties it depicts, it also lies in the confusion of markers between north and south, or between east and west. There are apples and pears in Flanders, just as there are in the Landes. There are strawberries near Brest and others by Marseille. A few culinary curiosities, such as the apples and pears "tapées," which are specialties of the Saumur region in western France, require some words of explanation for them to be understood today. Flattened then oven-dried, these autumnal delights could be preserved for several years, feeding sailors and protecting them effectively against nutritional deficiencies.

CARTE AGRICOLE
N° 2

GÉOGRAPHIE ÉCONOMIQUE ET AGRICOLE
LES BOISSONS : VIGNOBLES, PAYS A CIDRE ET A BIÈRE

Par Albert BERNARD
Instituteur
Officier de l'Instruction Publique

Beverages
–
Vineyards, Cider and Beer Regions

Agricultural map no. 2
Late nineteenth–
early twentieth century

"Economic and Agricultural Geography"
by Albert Bernard, schoolmaster
and public education officer
Éditions Les Fils d'Émile Deyrolle
46 rue du Bac, 7th arr., Paris
Imprimerie Gaillac-Monrocq & Cie

This map of France—crisscrossed with arrows, as though after a battle from another age—shows all its combinations of beverages. From north to south, and from east to west, both imports and exports display a most delightful exoticism. From Brazil, Jamaica, Egypt, Austria, and Britain, and ranging from coffee to rum to curacao, late nineteenth-century France set out to disprove the old adage that you die of thirst before you die of hunger.

Yet dating this map is not so simple. Signed by Albert Bernard, a schoolmaster born in 1851, it provides an overview of France's regions. History, however, tells of the turbulent destiny of Alsace and Lorraine, which shifted from France to Germany, then back again, from one war to the next. There is no suggestion of a border narrative here, which suggests an updating of agricultural data in the early 1920s. It is, above all, the consequences of the economic geography on the beverage consumption of the French that is being explored here.

The color code attributes yellow to the regions where grapes were grown, which immediately provides a vision of France's diversity in this respect. From Bordeaux to the Loire, from Champagne to Burgundy, and from the Midi to the Rhône, the country had been extensively planted with vines. A clear demarcation line between the north and the south can still be seen, showing that it was difficult to grow grapes anywhere to the north. But the large number of roads with the name "Rue des Vignes" (Vine Street) or bunches of grapes on stained-glass windows in churches might suggest the contrary. For, wherever there was a church, even north of the Loire, there was a small vineyard parcel, if only to satisfy the needs of the Sunday mass. Global warming could soon relaunch winegrowing in these regions, with the risk of competing with the traditional consumption of cider and beer.

PRÉSERVER LA BIODIVERSITÉ

LA RICHESSE VARIÉTALE

LE SAVIEZ-VOUS ?

• La tomate (*Solanum lycopersicum L.*) est un fruit de la famille des Solanacées, comme la pomme de terre, le piment, le poivron, l'aubergine et le physalis.
• Les bourdons savent détecter le pollen arrivé à maturité et peuvent jouer un rôle de fécondateur même si la tomate est en principe autogame (à la fois mâle et femelle).
• Le rouge de la tomate est dû à la présence dans l'épiderme du lycopène, une substance proche du carotène, qui aurait des vertus anti-cancérigènes.

LA TOMATE

MARMANDE

Variété précoce à mi-saison

Le fruit rouge, par grappes de 4 à 5 fruits, pèse de 150 à 250gr. Sa chair ferme, a une saveur sucrée et parfumée ; un vrai goût de tomate pour cette variété ancienne, originaire du Sud de la France à croissance vigoureuse et productive.

JAUNE À FARCIR

Variété de mi-saison

Fruit d'un beau jaune franc, ressemblant au poivron, de 80 à 90g, avec un intérieur creux, formant quatre cavités avec peu de graines. Son goût est doux et sa productivité moyenne.

MIRABELLA

Variété précoce

Fruit : orangé, petit – 20 à 25g – de type tomate cerise, en grappes très fournies. Son goût doux, légèrement sucré, fait de cette variété très productive une vraie gourmandise.

L'HYBRIDATION

La reproduction sexuée des tomates permet l'obtention d'une nouvelle variété. Dans cet exemple, le pollen d'une fleur de 'Green Zebra' déposé sur le pistil d'une fleur de 'Pink Berkeley Tie Dye' engendre une fécondation nouvelle appelée "Hybride". Cet hybride a été baptisé 'Belle du collège'. La migration du pollen (pollinisation) est possible grâce au vent, grâce à la main de l'homme mais surtout grâce aux insectes vibreurs tels que les bourdons.

NOIRE DE CRIMÉE

Variété semi-précoce

Fruit rouge brun très foncé, virant au noir aux extrémités. Juteux et doux il peut peser jusqu'à 500g. Originaire de Crimée.

CŒUR DE BŒUF JAPONAIS

Variété tardive

Fruit de couleur rose, pesant de 400 à 500g voire plus, dont la chair consistante offre une excellente saveur fruitée. Une variété qui se déguste nature.

CORNUE DES ANDES

Variété de mi-saison

Fruit d'un rouge franc, de la forme d'un piment pesant de 100 à 150g. Sa chair est ferme, avec peu de graines, et son goût excellent. Ne supporte pas bien l'excès d'arrosage.

ANANAS

Variété tardive

Fruit : rouge orangé, un peu côtelé et aplati vers le pédoncule, il peut peser jusqu'à 500g. Sa chair ferme, pulpeuse et juteuse, avec peu de graines, fait penser à celle de l'ananas. Son bel équilibre acide-sucré en fait une tomate d'un goût remarquable.

PRUNE NOIRE

Variété de mi-saison

Fruit : rouge-brun très foncé tirant sur le noir, de forme oblongue régulière se développe par grappes de 6 à 8 fruits de 25 à 30g. D'un goût doux et légèrement acide, sa productivité et sa résistance à l'éclatement sont bonnes. Originaire de Russie.

STRIPPED-CAVERN

Variété de mi-saison

Fruit : très beau, strié de rouge, jaune et orange, forme trois lobes bien distincts. Avec peu de graines et une chair douce, peu épaisse, cette tomate, assez vide, peut néanmoins peser environ 250g. Les fruits se conservent bien.

Dessins : Emmanuelle Étienne • © 2010 Éditions **DEYROLLE POUR L'AVENIR,** 46 rue du Bac – 75007 **PARIS** • www.deyrollepourlavenir.com

The Tomato

Educational plate
"Deyrolle for the Future"
no. 66
2010

From the series "Préserver la biodiversité – la richesse variétale" (Preserving biodiversity – species richness)
Éditions Deyrolle pour l'Avenir
46 rue du Bac, 7th arr., Paris

Nine of them have been honored by the artist Emmanuelle Étienne in this contemporary plate, published by Deyrolle pour l'Avenir (Deyrolle for the Future). Together, the Cornue des Andes, Mirabella, Black Crimean, Striped-Cavern, and their fellows celebrate the rich varieties of this fruit, which has been consumed since the sixteenth century in Europe. Louis Albert de Broglie, who has collected numerous examples, helped to create the Conservatoire National de la Tomate—housed since 1998 in the Château de la Bourdaisière, in the Indre-et-Loire department in west-central France—which displays with great affection the diversity of over 700 species that have been preserved there.

Long before they brightened up our summer dishes, tomatoes had a bad reputation. Small and round like a cherry, they were off-putting because of their similarity to the extremely toxic berry of the belladonna plant, found in open woodland. Originally from the lands of the Incas (they used to be called "apples of Peru"), they traveled via Spain, before making a name for themselves in Italy, where a few grafts and agronomical experiments were required to increase their volume. There is nothing like the yellow, black, green-striped, or scarlet flesh of a tomato, eaten in the garden, still warm from the sun. These fruits, which are 90 percent water, are by turn sweet, sharp, juicy, mild, fruity, fragrant, or indulgent. This plate devoted to them by Deyrolle makes the reader's mouth water, thanks to the accuracy and multiplicity of the descriptions.

Strangely, history tells us that tomatoes owe their development to the French Revolution. Their red color reflected the mood of the times but, more importantly, they were widely consumed in the South of France, long before they colonized Paris. This vegetable-fruit was well known to the cooks of Marseille, and when they marched up to Paris, singing La Marseillaise, they brought with them their fondness for tomatoes as well as the methods to prepare them. This culinary innovation subsequently prompted Parisian market-gardeners to begin growing them.

Text by
Emmanuelle Polle

Deyrolle

Louis Albert de Broglie
Owner

Francine Campa
CEO

Adèle Phelouzat
Director of Partnerships

Andréa Losi
Communications Manager

FLAMMARION
French Edition

Julie Rouart
Editorial Director

Delphine Montagne
Administration Manager

Mélanie Puchault
Editor

Roman Rolo
Designer

English Edition

Kate Mascaro
Editorial Director

Helen Adedotun
Editor

Translation from the French by
Ian Monk

Sarah Kane
Copyediting

Pierre-Yann Lallaizon / Studio Recto Verso
Typesetting

Nicole Foster
Proofreading

Corinne Trovarelli
Production

Les Artisans du Regard
Color Separation

Printed in Belgium by Graphius

Simultaneously published in French as
Deyrolle: Une Nature Nourricière
© Flammarion, S.A., Paris, 2020

English-language edition
© Flammarion, S.A., Paris, 2020

"Education through the eyes tires the intelligence less, but this education can have good results only if the ideas being inscribed on children's minds are strictly accurate."

Émile Deyrolle

Deyrolle's plates, whose precise dates of creation are debated, were produced between the second half of the nineteenth and the first half of the twentieth century. Aimed at different classes, from primary to secondary schools, and then for higher education, their vocation was to teach "practical lessons," but also botany, zoology, entomology, geography, human anatomy, civics, physics, chemistry, geology, mineralogy, biology, to name but a few. As of the end of the nineteenth century, several hundreds of subjects had been treated. Deyrolle thus became the primary supplier for public instruction, and he equipped schools with his educational plates and materials. Émile Deyrolle's publishing activity grew every year, and the creation of new educational plates continued. These plates even crossed borders, and were translated, in particular, into Spanish, Portuguese, and Arabic.

In 2007, Louis Albert de Broglie relaunched the publication of such educational plates: "After having explained the world to as many people as possible, the point now is to explain how to preserve it." This was the beginning of a new collection of educational plates (almost 150 in number) published under the name of Deyrolle pour l'Avenir (DPA), or "Deyrolle for the Future," which deal with contemporary environmental and societal issues.

Creating Your Home Gallery

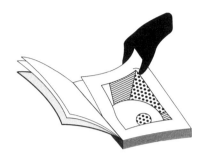

These prints can be framed effortlessly; they fit standard 9 × 12 in. or 24 × 30 cm frames (6 × 8 in. or 15 × 20 cm frames for the half-page prints). They also look attractive pinned to the wall with decorative thumb tacks.

For an attractive display, the works should ideally be placed 1¼ to 2 in. (3 to 5 cm) apart. Ensure the frames are equally spaced.

Alternate between portrait (vertical) and landscape (horizontal) formats for variety and harmony.

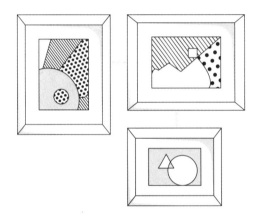

Align certain frames so as to create visual lines and add structure to the overall display.

Try distancing similar designs from each other to create additional visual interest.

The secret to creating a successful display is to establish interactions between key elements formed by colors or contours. A horizontal line will be the perfect counterpoint to a vertical motif, for example.

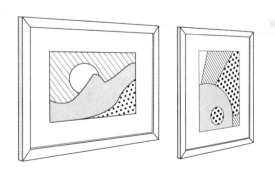

Changing the display regularly will instantly update your decor.